BOW &
BROMLEY-BY-BOW

GARY HAINES

The History Press

First published in 2008 by
The History Press
The Mill, Brimscombe Port,
Stroud, Gloucestershire, GL5 2QG
www.thehistorypress.co.uk

Reprinted in 2008

British Library Cataloguing in Publication Data
A catalogue record for this book is available from the British Library.

ISBN 978 0 7509 4791 6

*This book is dedicated to my Mum and Dad, Jean and Eric Haines, who give
everything and ask for nothing. I would not have been able to follow my passions for
history without their support and love. Thank you and love always.*

Bow Road, 1826. Of particular note is the water pump on the right-hand side. Development
was just beginning to creep into the area, as the houses on the road show.

Typesetting and origination by
The History Press.
Printed and bound in England.

CONTENTS

Number 40 Cardigan Road, Coronation Day, 3 June 1953. Terence J. Davis, in uniform, is standing at the dividing wall of Nos 38 and 40 with his mother, father and sisters.
(Photograph loaned by T.J. Davis to Tower Hamlets Local History Library and Archives)

INTRODUCTION

The two parishes of Bow and Bromley-by-Bow in London's East End have a long and distinct history although they have historically, and to some extent still do, struggle for identity. These parishes, linked as they are by industry and the River Lea, are located within the following geographical boundaries: Victoria Park to the north, River Lea to the east, Grove and Burdett Roads to the west and the Limehouse Cut to the south, which was created in 1770 to connect the Thames to the River Lea at Bromley-by-Bow. This, however, also cut Bromley in half, and south Bromley, which can be found south of the Limehouse Cut to East India Dock Road and from the River Lea on the east to approximately Chrisp Street in the west, is also represented in this book. These parishes were the site of great mansions and country retreats as well as industrial processes, including the largest dog biscuit factory in the world!

In 1664, 14,185 households were recorded in what is today the London Borough of Tower Hamlets: 2,482 in Whitechapel, 8,292 in locations near to the Thames east of the Tower of London down to Blackwall, 217 in Bethnal Green and only 175 in Bow and Old Ford. Bow, and particularly its neighbour Bromley-by-Bow, remained rural for much longer than other areas of the East End. 'Dear, charming beautiful Bromley . . . with its trees, its blackbirds and thrushes, its fields, its lovely gardens with their beautiful scents, its strawberries which I used to gather and eat.' So was the recollection of W.H. Fairburn, a resident of Bromley-by-Bow in the nineteenth century. The growth of the East End's population in the nineteenth century had a direct effect on the little villages dotted around the eastern outskirts, and many were swallowed up. Bow, which had a population of 2,500 in 1820, expanded gradually, but by 1908 its population had risen to 50,000.

The area that encompasses modern Bow was known by many names in the past, being termed 'Stratford' in 1177, 'Stratford ate Bowe' in 1279, 'Stratford at the Bowe' in 1494, 'Stratford the Bowe' in 1543, and 'Stratford Bowe' in 1547. 'Bowe' in 1594 is the earliest named reference where it is distinct from Stratford.

Bow is most famously linked with the story of Dick Whittington, who left London with his cat but was called back by the ringing of Bow bells. Although it is commonly thought that the church of St Mary-le-Bow in Cheapside was the location of these bells, a case has been made that St Mary's church in Bow Road may have been the source. Whittington may have been trading on the River Lea using coal barges to ship coal to the City from the north – these barges were also known as cats, hence the link with the mythical cat – and would have been within earshot of the bells in the church in Bow Road.

Bow itself originates from a settlement built on rising ground along the River Lea, and a bridge with bow-shaped arches that was built over this river. Bow was close to ancient crossing routes over this river and the Romans improved the crossing and constructed the London to Colchester road. This crossing became known as 'Old Ford'. Old Ford Road is now on the route that the Roman legions once took. Much archaeological evidence, including burials and pottery, serves as a witness to this time in Bow's history when Roman sandals marched across the area and the clatter of shields and swords could be heard.

In 1719 Bow became a parish in its own right. At this time Bow was still very much a rural retreat and remained that way throughout the eighteenth century. In 1795 it consisted of some 465 acres – 218 of these were arable, the rest were pasture and marshland. Around 200 years later Bow had grown to consist of 750 acres. This growth saw it expand into areas some residents would possibly argue are not in Bow. Tredegar Square is considered by many to be in Bow, although some would argue that historically this is in Mile End Old Town, hence its non-inclusion in this volume.

Bow's neighbour, Bromley-by-Bow, was originally described as the parish of Bromley St Leonard in reference to the priory and convent in the area. This parish covered some 475 acres and was situated along the east boundary of the London Borough of Tower Hamlets extending on a north-south line directly west of the River Lea for approximately one and a half miles. The area was also known simply as Bromley, but confusion with Bromley in Kent led to postal services calling it Bromley-by-Bow. The first use of this name can be found in 1786.

Bromley was named as 'Braembelege' in an Anglo-Saxon charter of about 1100. In 1274 it was known by the name 'Bromlegh', meaning 'woodland clearing where brambles grow' from the Old English 'braembel' and 'leah' reflecting its rural character. Chaucer refers to the medieval Bromley when he tells of his Prioress in the prologue to The Canterbury Tales as speaking French 'after the scole of Stratford ate Bowe' – a reference to the convent founded at Bromley.

This area changed drastically in the twentieth century with many buildings of historical and architectural interest surviving intact until the 1930s when they were demolished by London County Council's clearance programme, or they were destroyed in the Blitz. Railway development eliminated all remaining traces of rural Bromley, which had survived in the form of farmhouses and homesteads until 1850. The building of the Blackwall Tunnel Northern Approach Road in the late 1960s carved the landscape, industry, society and amenities in two and has led to it being one of the forgotten areas of East London in terms of its image, history and heritage.

Bow and Bromley parishes were absorbed into the Borough of Poplar in 1900. Poplar was one of three boroughs, along with Stepney and Bethnal Green, which were integrated in 1965 to form the London Borough of Tower Hamlets. The years to come will no doubt see more changes for Bow and Bromley-by-Bow as they border the River Lea, the other side of which will radically alter in the plans for Olympic regeneration and the Olympic Games ,due to take place in 2012. Such is the evolving nature of Bow and Bromley-by-Bow and of the East End itself.

This book is filled with the names of those who have been associated with Bow and Bromley-by-Bow, including George Lansbury, Annie Besant, Sylvia Pankhurst, Clara Grant and Mahatma Gandhi, to name but a few. All of these people had one thing in common; their desire to help and improve the lives of others. This book is a small tribute to them. It is with pride that I can state that I am, and always will be, a cockney lad from Bow.

All pictures come from the collection held at Tower Hamlets Local History Library and Archives unless otherwise stated.

Gary Haines, 2008

1

The Streets

Brunswick Road, looking north towards Bow, 1956. The pub on the left is the Cherry Tree. On the right is the war-damaged Emu House, premises of the Emu Wine Co. Ltd, which was rebuilt in 1958–9.

Above: This engraving published in September 1818 shows the diverse activities taking place around this ancient bridge which spanned the River Lea. A small dock can be seen which would have been used to load and unload goods. The bow shape of the bridge gave the parish of Bow its name.

The original Bow Bridge was erected in the twelfth century after Queen Matilda (Maud), wife of King Henry I, was nearly swept away with her retinue while crossing the river near Old Ford. Barking Abbey was responsible for the bridge's upkeep. A new bridge was built by the Turnpike Trust in 1839 in response to the increasing volume of traffic coming into the metropolis. The London County Council built a larger bridge but this too disappeared when the present Bow flyover, roundabout and northern approach to the Blackwall Tunnel was constructed in the 1960s.

William Kemp, a famous sixteenth-century Shakespearian comedy actor, laid a bet in 1599 that he could Morris dance from London to Norwich. He did so in nine days, setting off past Mile End and over Bow Bridge, then on to Stratford and finally Norwich, Morris dancing all the way!

Opposite below: An engraving of rural Bromley showing The Broadway in 1840. The Seven Stars Inn – which is now residential housing – can be traced back to 1681, and was located on the corner of Bromley High Street and St Leonard's Street (known as the Pearly Kings and Queens in the 1980s). The origin of the inn's sign has many explanations. It may be based on the sign for seven planets, Jupiter, Saturn, Mercury, Venus, Mars, the Sun and the Moon. The sign may also have its associations with the Book of Revelation; the seven stars of the seven churches. The inn sign is also often associated with bridges.

Above: An engraving of Bow Bridge by W. Bartlett, published in 1832. This engraving gives a good impression, albeit a romantic one, of what the village of Bow was like at this time.

'The Poplars', Old Ford, 1817, from a painting by Henry Matthews, who lived here in the early 1800s. Matthews was an East India Co. employee and died in 1830. His family are depicted here playing battledore and shuttlecock in front of the house, which was later incorporated into the site of Bryant & May's match factory.

KING JOHN'S PALACE, OLD FORD

King John's Palace, Old Ford, taken from a print *c.* 1863. This engraving shows on the right a twelve-roomed residence that was reputedly part of a mansion known as King John's Palace, located in Wick Lane. The building stood on a terrace and had a large oak staircase. At one time the residence was famous as a hostelry but the building of Bow Bridge changed the route into Essex and trade died away. The residence was destroyed by fire on Wednesday 23 September 1863. Little else is known about this mansion or its connections, if any, to royalty.

Bromley Palace, St Leonard's Street, from a painting by Stourton L. Needham, 1853–4. The origins of this building can be traced back to James I who possibly built it as a hunting lodge. The state room featured the arms, motto, crest and initials of the king. The palace was altered in 1750 and became two residences. This building then became Palace House School at some point after this date. The building itself by all accounts was beautifully decorated inside with elaborate plaster ceilings, pilastered panelling, a fireplace and overmantel with royal arms. This beautiful historic building was acquired by the School Board for London and demolished in 1893 to make way for a new school. This caused great protests at the time and was the subject of a survey by the newly formed Survey of London who could do nothing but record this as one of seventeen historic buildings in the parish. By the time the survey was published in 1900, four other buildings had disappeared forever. The leader of this new organisation, the architect C.R. Ashbee, wrote in his introduction to the survey of the palace, 'It is useless to cry over spilt milk, but if the destruction of what, in a sense, was the finest building in East London did nothing else, it at least awakened the public conscience and was the immediate cause of the founding of the Committee for the Survey of the Memorials of Greater London, under whose auspices this monograph, this third of the series is now presented.' C.R. Ashbee goes on to call the demolishing of the palace 'this most shameless piece of destruction'.

A fireplace from Bromley Palace, 1916. Some items from the palace were rescued before its demolition and were placed on display in the Victoria and Albert Museum in the Bromley-by-Bow room. A ground-floor room of the palace can still be seen at the museum and is displayed with furnishings made between 1550 and 1620. The Victoria and Albert Museum does, however, dispute the link with James I, arguing that the Royal Arms over the mantle of the fireplace could be evidence that the owner was not entitled to his own coat of arms and may indicate that the palace was the second home of a courtier or wealthy merchant rather than a member of the royal family.

Bromley Hall, Gillender Street, *c.* 1912. This Grade II listed two-storey building may have been part of a manor house and is the oldest surviving building in the area – tree-rings date some of the timbers in the building to about 1490. One of the more notable people to have lived here was William Cecil, later Lord Burghley, who was appointed Secretary of State by Elizabeth I in 1558. The building was damaged by bombing in 1940 and repaired in 1951. The hall has had various uses throughout the years. In the eighteenth century, the site was used in the production of calico due to its location near the River Lea. The Regions Beyond Missionary Union occupied the hall from 1894–1914. The Royal College of St Katherine then took over the hall, using it as a welfare centre for infants. It was also the private residence of the manager of a nearby carpet warehouse. A preservation order was placed on the hall in 1951 ensuring the building's survival. In March 2005 a £1m restoration project was embarked on by Leaside Regeneration, English Heritage and Tower Hamlets Council, and in 2007, London Assembly members visited the hall to view a good example of how listed buildings can be regenerated and adapted for local community use.

Bromley Hall, *c.* 1930. Katherine Blount, Lady in Waiting to King Henry VIII's first wife, Catherine of Aragon, lived here and would have wandered around the gardens. It may also have been here that the King met Elizabeth Blount, Katherine's teenage daughter, who was known for her beauty. Elizabeth, also known as Bessie, bore Henry his much wanted son in 1519, naming him Henry Fitzroy, but his illegitimacy meant he could not lawfully become King of England after his father's reign ended. Henry Fitzroy died in 1536. After their affair ceased, the King then embarked on an affair with Lady Mary Boleyn, who was then replaced in Henry's affections by her sister Anne, whom he decided to marry.

Workmen's Home, Bow Road, *c.* 1928. This building originally stood on the north side of Bow Road. It was built in about 1600 and was remodelled in about 1700 when it was given a modern front. In 1612 it was said to be the residence of Lord Sheffield, who took part in fighting the Spanish Armada. The building was demolished in 1929.

Bow Bridge, looking east, *c.* 1912. Coming over the bridge can be seen a West Ham Corporation tramcar.

Bow Road, *c.* 1900. The premises of the Bow and Bromley Liberal and Radical Association can be seen in the centre.

The only identifiable surviving feature from this view of Bow Road in 1899 is the triangular shaped rooftops on the far left of the photograph. Next door to this house in 1902 (on the right) was 177 Bow Road, the premises of the Bow and Bromley branch of the Social Democratic Federation. The ironmonger's at 201 Bow Road had disappeared by 1906.

Bow Road in 1951, showing shop nos 126–141. Also in this picture can be viewed the ancestry of the author. The author's mum, Jean Haines, worked for nearly nine years in a pie and mash shop based in Roman Road while his dad, Eric Haines, worked for over thirteen years for Truman's Brewery based in Brick Lane.

Looking east to Fairfield Road Corner, Bow Road and Bow Church. The top of the church tower of St Mary's can just be seen behind the trees. The order was given to construct Fairfield Road on 5 February 1875. It replaced Carlisle Terrace, Harrold Terrace, William Terrace, Plant Terrace, Railway Cottages, Grove Hall Terrace, Hermitage Terrace, Catherine Terrace, Friedrich Cottages and Fairfield Cottages. The building on the corner is now the National Westminster Bank. *(Postcard loaned to Tower Hamlets Local History Library and Archives by Mr Philip Mernick)*

Fairfield Road with rather less traffic than now, *c.* 1905. The fashions of the early twentieth century are clearly on display. *(Photograph loaned to Tower Hamlets Local History Library and Archives by Revd A.R. Royall)*

Corner of Bow Road and Campbell Road, *c.* 1911. C.E. Yorke & Son, Coal Merchants and Factors Ltd, was in business at 88 Bow Road between 1911 and 1918. Gentlemen are waiting to take a delivery of coal at what appears to be the sales entrance of the premises. The London and South Western Bank Ltd was located at nos 90 and 92 Bow Road. In 1902 the manager was an aptly named Mr Octavius E. Riche.

Bow Road looking towards Addington Road, *c.* 1915. The man nonchalantly walking across Bow Road by the tramlines would today surely be running frantically for his life across this now busy thoroughfare. Tower Hamlets Council is currently in the early stages of devising a tramway scheme along a new boulevard, using Whitechapel Road and Bow Road and leading to the London 2012 Olympic Park. The large building on the left is Bow police station. The railway bridge across Bow Road featured in the opening title sequence for *The Bill* television series in the 1980s and '90s.

Right: Looking east through an arch of the old Great Eastern Railway bridge, Bow Road, 1953. The bridge opened on 29 December 1848.

Electric House, Bow Road, on the corner of Alfred Street, *c.* 1930. Purchase of the land on which Electric House was built was delayed for a time due to possible plans to erect a cinema. A direct approach to the landowner, Lord Tredegar, finally secured the site and work commenced on 25 February 1924. The building was opened on 29 May 1925 at a cost of £31,000 and contained flats, a showroom for the council's electricity department and four shops on the ground floor. Costs of design were kept to a minimum although purple dorking facing bricks were used on the front elevations. In many ways the building was a showpiece for the socialists and the Poplar Council and Board of Guardians of the time. It was reported in the *East London Advertiser* that 'The Mayor, [Edgar Lansbury] in introducing Mr John Wheatley [who was to open the building] said they heard a great deal of criticism about socialists and their theories and how the Poplar Council and the Board of Guardians were all right with their talk, but when it came to putting theory into practise did not know how to get on with the job. That evening, however, they were assembled around one of the jobs . . . that they had got on with!' Electric House was seen as a significant step in solving the housing problem in the Borough of Poplar and when opened, the council had completed the building of 465 flats and houses. The clock on the front of the building was made from wrought iron and has three faces. The Minnie Lansbury Memorial Clock, as it was called, was named after the first wife of Edgar Lansbury, eldest son of George.

Minnie Lansbury, suffragette, socialist and councillor, was born in Whitechapel in 1889 and was one of thirty councillors, five of them women, sent to prison in September 1921 during the Poplar Rates Dispute. As Alderman of Poplar Council, she was jailed, along with George Lansbury, as one of the thirty Labour 'rebel' councillors who made a stand against the government by refusing to raise the borough's tax rate due to their belief in the unfairness of a system which meant that the poorest borough's had to pay the same rate as the wealthiest. When Poplar Council decided to stop collecting rates for outside bodies, these thirty councillors were jailed after they marched five miles to the Law Courts in the Strand on 29 July 1921 to put forward their case. The men were sent to Brixton prison, where George Lansbury would address the crowds through the bars of his cell, and the women to Holloway. Minnie contracted pneumonia and died on 1 January 1922, six weeks after her release from prison, at the age of 32. Thousands of East Enders lined the streets for her funeral. She was honoured for her heroism with this memorial clock. During an appeal for funds to restore the clock in April 2007, the most famous bearer of the Lansbury surname today, Angela Lansbury, daughter of Edgar Lansbury, donated funds towards its repair. Among its functions, the clock serves as a knowledge point for those trying to memorise the streets of London for their prestigious Cab badge.

St Leonard's Road viewed from East India Dock Road, looking towards Bromley, 1904. The pub on the left at No. 279, with a police officer standing outside keeping a wary eye on things, was to become the Sir John Franklin. The shop on the right is Lewis, Nevis and Co., Linen Drapers. *(Postcard loaned to Tower Hamlets Local History Library and Archives by Mr Philip Mernick)*

Looking south-west along the north end of St Leonard's Road, by Venue Street, *c.* 1925. Spratt's factory can be seen in the background. This factory, built in orange brick, was constructed around 1899 and manufactured pet food, kennels etc. Barges would travel along the canal delivering fish heads, which would be turned into pet food. James Spratt, the founder, went from selling lightning rods to selling commercial dog biscuits, believing these would be healthier for dogs than being fed scraps and leftovers. The factory closed in the 1960s but is still a major landmark in the area. Once described as 'the largest [factory] in the world' it is now offices, flats and artists' studios.

Looking north-east along St Leonard's Road, 1956. Drew Street is on the right.

St Leonard's Road, by Wyvis Street, *c.* 1926. Bartlett Street is on the extreme left. The derelict building (No. 305) was for many years owned by the East London Wharf and Warehouse Co., Wharfingers. A block of flats is now on this site.

St Leonard's Street, Bromley-by-Bow, by Three Mill Lane and looking towards Bow
Bridge, 1937. St Leonard's Street was at one time the main street in Bromley-by-Bow.
The rather ornate lamppost in the background on the left can still be viewed in St
Leonard's Street.

Looking north along St Leonard's Street towards the recreation ground and Old Palace
School, 1956.

Above: Looking south along Bromley High Street toward Devon's Road, *c.* 1927. A collection of shops and residences, this street included in 1927 Mrs Emma Harriot Ayton, tobacconist at No. 2, a boot repairer at No. 4 and Mrs Sarah Harniman, florist at No. 6. Opposite these shops, perhaps directly behind the photographer, could be found Mrs Alice Morris' coffee rooms at No. 3, John Miller, furniture dealer at No. 5 and Morris Wintinsky, baker at No. 7. Another coffee room was present at No. 9.

Left: Baker's Alley, Bromley High Street, *c.* 1930. This alley has been demolished.

Looking north along Devon's Road, at the junction with Bromley High Street, 1964. Road widening has seen this area change dramatically. Bromley High Street at one time had a village green and blacksmiths. Near its green was located a ducking stool, whipping post and stocks until the 1850s. The Rose and Crown pub was a nineteenth-century building which replaced the Bowling Green Inn. This was located, perhaps not surprisingly, on one corner of the village bowling green. This road may have received its name from one Thomas Devon who is listed in the poor rate for 1721. The earliest mention of this street can be found in the Bromley poor rate for March 1790; at this time the street was shown on maps as Bromley Lane. This lane was also known as Devon's Lane, which was renamed Devon's Road by the mid-nineteenth century. *(Photograph donated to Tower Hamlets Local History Library and Archives by Mr Gardner, Chief Officer, Public Control, 1968)*

Old Ford Road, looking west. In the foreground on the left can be seen the premises of the Royal Victor pub at No. 234. On the right in the background can be seen the Royal Cricketers at No. 211.

Old Ford Road, with Iceland Road on the left, 1934. This is the site of Edgar House, erected in 1935. The houses in Maverton Road have the obligatory lines of washing hanging out to dry!

Old Ford Road taken from Duckett's Canal Bridge, looking west from Skew Bridge. The road on the right is Driffield Road. Rather intriguingly, the postcard has a Toronto, Canada postmark.

A row of terraced houses in Tomlin's Grove, *c.* 1907. Tomlin's Grove is named after Thomas Tomlin, a landowner in Bromley-by-Bow and a retired East India Co. captain and a Justice of the Peace. In December 1913, Tomlin's Grove saw bloodshed when a suffragette march led by Zelie Emerson went to 13 Tomlin's Grove, the house of councillor John Le Manquais who had voted in favour of excluding suffragettes from council property. Tomlin's Grove was blocked off at both ends by mounted police, and policemen on foot broke up the demonstration with truncheons, resulting in many serious injuries. *(Postcard loaned to Tower Hamlets Local History Library and Archives by Mr Philip Mernick)*

Boys pose for the camera in an almost traffic-free Coborn Road, *c.* 1907. The corner of Malmsbury Road is on the right. Number 62 is on the right with higher even-numbered houses in the distance. Before 1800, this road was known as Cut Throat Lane, perhaps an indication of a rather shady past. *(Postcard loaned to Tower Hamlets Local History Library and Archives by Mr Philip Mernick)*

Bow Road viewed from Coborn Street junction, March 1962. Bow Road Methodist Church can be seen on the left.

Tredegar Road, with Balmer Road on the right, *c.* 1890. The sender of this postcard writes: 'For dear Susan, I live down where the two children are standing and my house is just the same as the one where they are – I get my Reid's Stout at the little pub opposite that you can see.' Sadly, the writer has not signed the postcard.

Above: The North London Railway bridge, Tredegar Road, *c.* 1955. This bridge was constructed under an Act of Parliament of 1846 and opened in 1850.

Opposite below: Roman Road, Old Ford. An early forerunner of the alas, now vanished Routemaster number 8 bus travels along Roman Road towards Old Ford and Bow Church. The impressive steeple belonged to St Barnabas Church which stood on the corner of Roman Road and Grove Road, Bethnal Green. Damaged by bombing during the Second World War, this spire was removed and the remaining steeple capped. Much of the church was rebuilt in 1956–7.

Above: Bow Road, 1905. Tredegar House, on the left, was erected on land owned by Lord Tredegar. The original occupants were Joseph Westwood and family in the mid-1800s. Joseph made his fortune as a shipbuilder and iron bridge builder at Millwall. In 1893, a training school for nurses was opened here and the First World War heroine, Edith Cavell attended in 1895. While working as a matron in Belgium, she was accused by the Germans of being a spy after British soldiers were captured on their way to the border. She was executed in October 1915 after making no defence at her trial, at which it was noted that she 'spoke without trembling and showed a clear mind'. Edith Cavell possibly helped hundreds of British and French patients to escape to the neutral Netherlands from Belgium. Many memorials now remember her heroism, one of the most significant and moving being adjacent to Trafalgar Square located near to the National Portrait Gallery in London. In 1912, Tredegar House and the adjoining property were demolished and a new building was constructed as a school for nurses and opened by Queen Alexandra on 12 July 1912. The school was closed in the 1970s and Tredegar House is now residential.

A child stands on a demolition site after the Second World War bombing of Thistle House and Heather House, Brunswick Road, 1955. Houses in Ettrick Street can be seen on the left. In the background, on the far right of the photograph can be seen the Church of St Nicholas and All Hallows, Aberfeldy Street, which opened in October 1955. Bomb sites remained unofficial recreation grounds for children until redevelopment took place. Reconstruction was in many cases anything but instantaneous, as this photograph shows.

St Paul's Way, looking east towards the junction of Bow Common Lane, 1941. Selsey Street and the spire of Holy Name Church are in the background. It is easy when looking at photographs of bomb-damaged buildings to forget the human cost of war. Rose Stovell, aged 50, of No. 1 Selsey Street, Mary Lane, aged 53, of 37 Selsey Street and Albert Blake, aged 16, of No. 4 Selsey Street all died in a bombing raid here on 7 September 1940. This was the first night of the Blitz and the first of fifty-seven consecutive nights of bombing in London.

Bow Common Lane on the corner of Devon's Road, *c.* 1950. The sign indicates the Moors Arms, which was at 28 Bow Common Lane.

A van from the John Lewis department store travels along a deserted Fairfield Road in 1955. The factory on the right is A. Baveystock & Co. Ltd, children's cot manufacturers.

A glimpse of rural Bow, nos 2–3 Lefevre Grove (now Nos 4–5 Tamar Cottages), June 1966.

Lefevre Road on the corner with Tredegar Road, 20 November 1969. The nineteenth-century terraces on Lefevre Road have disappeared to make way for new residential housing. The pub on the corner is the Bridge House.

Children gather outside a house in Alfred Street, *c.* 1905. *(Postcard loaned to Tower Hamlets Local History Library and Archives by Mr Philip Mernick)*

Archibald Street, looking east from Wellington Way, April 1968. Wellington Way derives its name from William Wellesley, nephew of the Duke of Wellington, who at one time resided in Bow Road.

Armagh Road, looking north towards Roman Road, 1956. Armagh Road is first noted on a plan of 1855. Rosedell Terrace, a long forgotten street in Bow, was incorporated into Armagh Road by order of the Metropolitan Board of Works in March 1871. *(Photograph copied from original in possession of T.J. Davis)*

Parnell Road, Bow, 1970. Due to changes in the area in the 1980s and '90s, this style of houses – and car models – will not be seen again.

Looking north along Gunmaker's Lane, October 1965. This lane is so called as it once led to the London Small Arms Co. which was situated at the canal wharf from 1867–1919. During the First World War this company produced up to 2,000 rifles a week. The location near the canal was also advantageous as it provided the link to the Royal Small Arms Factory in Enfield where armaments produced at the London Small Arms Co. were tested. Following extensive redevelopment in 1999–2001, stylish flats now dominate this area.

Above: Old Ford Road, west of the junction with Parnell Road, looking south towards the newly built Annie Besant Close housing estate, May 1980.

Left: Tredegar Road, near Parnell Road, January 2007. This photograph captures another phase in the ever-changing history of the streets of Bow and Bromley-by-Bow. This new development of one and two bedroom apartments is built on the former site of Lefevre Walk. *(Donated by Gary Haines to Tower Hamlets Local History Library and Archives)*

2

Shopping & Industry

Banana stall, Roman Road market, 1946. The stallholder was Mr Michael Goldberg, who was known locally as the 'Banana King'. Mr Goldberg lived in Monier Road, Bow, and died in 1958. *(Original photograph given to Robert Anthony photographers by Rita Goldberg, daughter of Michael Goldberg)*

Ye Olde Bow, *c.* 1912. This shop, which offered 'tea and light refreshment rooms', was situated on the south side of Bow Road, opposite St Mary's Church on the corner of Brewery Yard. It is possible that some of these refreshments may have been served in Bow porcelain, for which the area was widely famed in the mid-eighteenth century. Manufacturing began in an existing glass factory in 1744 by Thomas Frye who discovered a new way to make porcelain. Later, a second factory was opened on the Stratford, Essex side of the River Lea. This factory was known as 'New Canton' and was most productive in the 1750s, but production ceased in 1776. Many wares were produced, including statuettes in porcelain, tableware, bowls and vases.

Right: J.H. George, the old shoemaker's shop, at 4 Bromley High Street near the corner of High Street and Bow Road, 1946. This seventeenth-century shop front was gabled and weather-boarded. The building was demolished in February 1959.

Below: The Sun Flour Mills, Bromley-by-Bow, *c.* 1910. On the right can be seen part of Walmsley's Maltings, now demolished. In May 1952 a fire broke out and burned for two hours, destroying part of the mill.

Construction of part of the main Metropolis drainage system, the *Illustrated London News*,
27 August 1859. This is a sectional view of the tunnels from Wick Lane, near Old Ford,
Bow, looking westward. In the summer of 1858, the polluting sewage in the Thames was
so odorous that it forced Members of Parliament to leave the House of Commons. *The Times*
dubbed this 'The Great Stink'. The famous engineer, and arguably the man responsible for
saving countless generations of Londoners from death and disease, Sir Joseph Bazelgette, was
given the task of improving the sewage system. Bazelgette built a series of sewers, pumping
stations and treatment works, many of which still serve London today.

Old Ford Lock, River Lea, 1966. This lock was opened in 1866 to help the transport of goods from factories based on the riverside. Many thousands of tons of merchandise have made their way through these locks. The River Lea flows from its source in Bedfordshire to join the Thames at Bow Creek. By tradition, it marks the boundary between Middlesex and Essex, with Bow and Bromley-by-Bow being in the old county of Middlesex.

Lea Navigation Canal, 1975. Old Ford Lock can be seen in the background. In the seventeenth and eighteenth centuries, dyeing and calico industries would use the canal water at Bow in their manufacturing processes.

The north side of Bow Bridge, *c.* 1912. The premises of J.W. French and Co., Millers, are on the right.

Devine & Co., Whalebone Cutters, St Stephens Road, Old Ford, in the 1920s. Manager William Stanway is wearing an overall, third from the left. In the 1930s, this firm was advertising itself as being the oldest of its trade in the country. Whalebone had many uses including being used in brushes and brooms, belts, corsets and surgical instruments. *(Photograph loaned to Tower Hamlets Local History Library and Archives by Mr A.J. Moody)*

Right: E.T. Taylor, Wholesale and Retail Tobacconist, at 108 Bow Road, 1952. A bewildering range of tobacco and accessories can be viewed in the Neo-Victorian style shop windows.

Below: E.T. Taylor also owned a stationery shop, located next door to the tobacconist. The two shops were located at 108–110 Bow Road. The stationery shop premises at No. 110 were formerly used as a Citizen's Advice Bureau by Pilgrim House before their conversion into a shop in 1952.

Left: J. Masters, Watch Maker and Jeweller at 22 St Leonard's Street, Bromley, 1909.

Below: Looking south along St Leonard's Street, Bromley-by-Bow, in the 1940s. There is a puzzle regarding the exact date this photograph was taken. In 1908 Charles Rogers, boot and shoemaker, was at 197 St Leonard's Street. Between about 1911 and 1940 Emma Grace Bernard, confectioner, was trading at this address. The confectioner's is not traceable after 1940. Therefore one could state that this photograph dates from about 1940.

Addington Road, 1907. In 1898 a stationer's was present on this site, run by Edward Brown, which was replaced by A.C. Crowder in the early 1900s. Alfred Charles Crowder seems to have changed the business, being listed in the trade directories as a motorcar agent in 1937. The premises had disappeared from the listings by 1942.

Numbers 641–5 Roman Road in the 1960s. A Mr H. Pittock remembers that before Denny and Holland took over the shop at 643 Roman Road it was Short's, run by Mr Short and his sister. They managed an old-fashioned oil-shop, which used to have biblical texts scattered around the shelves. The range of stock was vast. If you wanted anything, the usual answer was to 'go to Short's'. The Gentlemen's Hairdressing premises on the corner of Appian Road were once Owens, the undertakers. (*Photograph donated to Tower Hamlets Local History Library and Archives by Mr H. Pittock*)

Left: Wolf Cohen, tailor, at 256 Roman Road, *c.* 1904. These premises opened in April 1904.

Below: C.H. Ealsea, Tobacconist and Newsagent at 69 Devon's Road, *c.* 1911. *(Photograph donated to Tower Hamlets Local History Library and Archives by Mr Hawkes)*

The old corn chandler's shop at 223 Bow Road, 1937. At this time, the shop was owned by Thomas Stanley Howes. Next door, at No. 221, were the premises of William's Ben and Co. Ltd, Wholesale Clothing Manufacturers, and to the right was Bow Baptist Church. The Howes were a well-established family in the area. In 1861, Thomas Howes was a corn dealer in premises in the High Street, Bow, and in 1889, Mrs Mary Howes was a corn dealer at 223 Bow Road. The Howes family continued to run the corn chandlers until 1959 when Robson J. & Son, credit drapers, occupied the premises. By this time, presumably the trade for 'Hay at 2/6' and 'Best Horse Mixture' had declined. In the late 1970s and throughout the 1980s, Ye Olde-Style Confectionery sweet manufacturers were located on these premises.

Roman Road market, May 1970.
The only business recognisable
today is Barclays Bank. The market
has a reputation as an excellent
place from which to buy clothes
– as the number of stalls selling
fashion in this photograph testifies.

Roman Road market, known by locals as the 'Roman', *c.* 1969. The market started in about 1843 and once saw suffragettes running a stall selling jumble and the *Women's Dreadnought* – their campaign newspaper – to raise funds. Sylvia Pankhurst wrote most of the articles but other writers also contributed on occasion, including George Lansbury.

Roman Road market in full flow on a market day, viewed from Parnell Road, 1981. The main market days are Saturdays, Tuesdays and Thursdays. To earn their living, stallholders will often be found at other markets on other days of the week.

Number 69 Roman Road at the junction with Vivian Road, *c.* 1935. These premises were known for over seventy years as the location of Rickards umbrella shop, which was founded in 1859 by Mr Richard Rickards. The business thrived until 1935 when Richard's son, Albert, sold the premises to concentrate on a shop also selling umbrellas in Leytonstone. The premises were converted into the Roman Road Branch Library. This building was bombed during the Second World War and a temporary hut was built on the site and continued to serve as a library. This small building, which held the last Roman Road Branch Library, was demolished in 2007.

Messrs J. Evershed and Co., printers in Bow, 1947. Large quantities of paper can be seen in the background of this photograph, which shows the printing presses at work.

'The Match-Makers at the East-End' illustration from *The Graphic*, 20 May 1871. In 1860, William Bryant and Francis May found a 3 acre site in Fairfield Road, which contained an abandoned crinoline factory, a candle making company and a rope works. It was here that the match factory was built, designed by Johan Lundstrom. In 1888 Annie Besant, a journalist and member of the Fabian Society, investigated working conditions in the factory and published an article entitled 'White Slavery in London'. This was based on discussions with the workers in the factory who spoke of the working conditions. Due to exposure to phosphorous, which was used to make the match heads, many workers suffered yellowing of the skin, hair loss and 'phossy jaw'; a form of bone cancer in the mouth that lead to the whole side of the face turning green and black, and to lethal poisoning. When two of the girls who had spoken to Annie Besant were promptly sacked, Annie distributed leaflets around the factory calling for a strike and 1,200 women and girls answered the call. Celebrities of the time, including George Bernard Shaw, supported them and marches, and demonstrations took place in Victoria Park, Mile End and Hyde Park. On 21 July 1888, the strike was called off and Annie Besant formed the Union of Matchmakers. Concessions were made by Bryant & May to their workers. Annie Besant is remembered today in the form of Annie Besant Close, a housing estate in Bow.

Interior of the Bryant & May match factory, Fairfield Road, *c.* 1968. This photograph shows the output side of a match-making machine. Dried matches are moved down towards the inner boxes, as can be seen on the right of the photograph. The outer boxes move down to the inner part of the matchbox, which is then slid into them. The closed boxes then pass along the inspection conveyor belt and finally onto the wrapping machine. *(Photograph donated to Tower Hamlets Local History Library and Archives by Anthony Blake)*

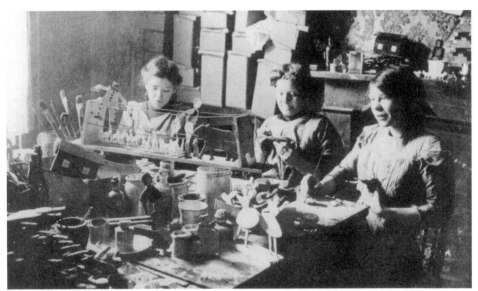

Suffragettes making toys at their factory at 45 Norman Grove, Bow, *c.* 1915. Some of these toys may have made their way onto the stall the suffragettes used to run in Roman Road market. This property was also a boot and clothing factory, a crèche and a nursery. The crèche charged 3*d*, including food, and was soon oversubscribed. The toy factory provided work at realistic wages for women whose options were limited and had children to look after. Wages were a minimum of 5*d* an hour and the workers could choose their own hours. The factory struggled to make a profit when other manufacturers copied their popular toys. The factory remained at Norman Grove until 1934, when it moved to King's Cross where it was bombed in 1943 during the Blitz. *(Photograph originally published in Home Front by Sylvia Pankhurst)*

'View near Bromley Mill,' an illustration of the Tide Mill, Three Mills Lane,
by J. Hitchins, 1826. These tide mills in London were unique as they were
situated further from the sea than any other tide mill in Britain. This mill
would have used the ebb of the tide as a means of power for the grain
distillery. The Clock Mill's corner tower is faced in brick and has Gothic
windows which date from 1817. The timber-framed House Mill dates from
1776. The third mill, which would have stood on this site, was demolished by
Edward VI to improve traffic along the River Lea. Although many people think
that Three Mills is situated in Bromley-by-Bow, they are actually within the
boundaries of Newham. The mills are the last remaining tide mills in London
and are now managed as a heritage site.

The Walmsley's Maltings, Bromley-by-Bow, 1934. The Walmsley's Maltings,
which had been in operation for a hundred years, was purchased by the
London County Council in 1934. The Coventry Cross Estate, now demolished,
was built on the site. The name 'Coventry Cross' originated from a tavern that
existed in 1690 when the area saw a 'beating the bounds' ceremony and the
Coventry Cross tavern laid on a lavish dinner for the procession.

Above: H.W. Mobbs, pawnbrokers at
93 St Leonard's Street, 1924. Fred
Munk, Harold Mobbs' assistant, is in
the doorway. *(Photograph donated to
Tower Hamlets Local History Library
and Archives by G.E. Mobbs)*

Right: Number 529 Roman Road,
c. 1954. This shop appears to be
two shops in one: Maison Henry's:
For Better Perms, and Bow Radio
Supplies. However, the top sign has
evaded obliteration from whitewashes
and dates from the previous
incumbent. A hairdresser had been
operating on these premises since the
late 1890s. In 1952, Maison Henry's
became Bow Radio Supplies and only
four years later became Bow Record
Centre. A record shop remained on
these premises until 1979. In 1981,
Shoe Tree ladies' shoe shop opened.
Today, the Shu-Boyz, specialists
in ladies' and children's footwear,
continues the tradition of a shoe shop
on these premises next door to The
Trader, formally the Needle Gun pub.

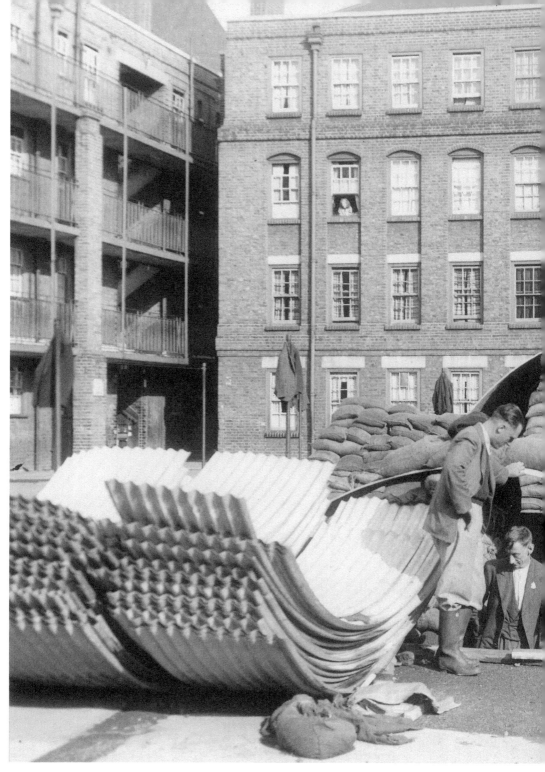

Constructing an air-raid shelter at Sumner House, Maddams Street, Bromley-by-Bow, 1939.
Poplar Council estimated that about 3,608,000 sandbags were needed to prepare the
borough for the outbreak of war.

Spratt's, a well-known manufacturer of animal foods based in Bromley-by-Bow, supplied a novelty exhibit for Poplar's carnival on 6 June 1953. Before 1914, Spratt's factory also manufactured food for human consumption. During the Boer War, the factory produced about four million biscuits a week, which were used to supply the British Army.

Children play against the side of Groves in Stafford Road, 1965. C. Groves, Tobacconist and Confectioner, was first established at 43 Saxon Road in 1938. At this time, Saxon Road had among its traders a mantle maker at No. 7, a sawdust contractor at No. 29 and a dairy belonging to one Herbert Honeyball at No. 98. It is perhaps no surprise when looking at this picture to discover that C. Groves had closed by 1968.

3

Places of Alcoholic Refreshment

Bromley Hall tavern, 211 Brunswick Road, with Zetland Road on the right, pre-1971. This public house existed from about 1902 to 1971 when Brunswick Road was widened to make way for the Blackwall Tunnel Northern Approach Road. The pub was named after the manor house that was located here in Tudor times. *(Photograph loaned to Tower Hamlets Local History Library and Archives by Truman's Brewery)*

Left: Brewery Yard, Bow, looking towards Bow Road, *c.* 1912. On the left can be seen the rear of Ye Olde Bow shop.

Below: Looking east along Bow Road, *c.* 1907. The White Horse pub can be seen on the right at 214 Bow Road. At a vestry meeting in Bromley St Leonard on 10 May 1838, an assessment was made of the public houses in the area. The following names were listed, many of which have now disappeared: Lord Nelson, Dock House, Grave Maurice, Cherry Tree, Five Bells, Coventry Cross, Mulberry Tree, Imperial Crown, Seven Stars, Fishing Boat, Rose and Crown, Bird in the Hand and the More's Arms. *(Postcard loaned to Tower Hamlets Local History Library and Archives by Mr Philip Mernick)*

Bow Brewery, Bromley High Street. This brewery was demolished in 1933 and replaced with Bradley House, a block of flats. The brewery had been in existence for a number of years prior to its rebuilding in 1821. The London of the 1370s is praised by Chaucer in his *Canterbury Tales* for its 'pot of London ale'. At one time London had some 120 breweries. Many of these would have been sited near to the Thames where they would be able to obtain their supplies of barley and malt from East Anglia and hops from Kent via barges. They would also draw their water supply from the river.

The Zimmermann family and employees pose outside the City Arms, 134 Devon's Road, *c.* 1904. The proprietor, W. Zimmermann, was born in Germany in about 1865. His wife, Caroline, was born in St George's in the East End in about 1866, and their daughter Annie was born in Mile End in 1898. 'Holt and Co.'s Entire', advertised on the top of the building, marks the ownership. The brewery was located at 52 Broad Street, Ratcliff, until about 1912. *(Postcard loaned to Tower Hamlets Local History Library and Archives by Mr Philip Mernick)*

The St Leonard's Arms, 162 St Leonard's Road. This photograph can be dated from 1934–52 as it was in this period that Thomas William Mercer was publican. A public house has been on this site since 1859 when one James Morris was landlord. When Dewberry Street was realigned at the junction of St Leonard's Road, the pub became part of a traffic island. The building has since been converted into nine flats. *(Photograph loaned to Tower Hamlets Local History Library and Archives by Truman's Brewery)*

Bird in the Hand, 126 Bow Road. The name is based on the proverb, 'A bird in the hand is worth two in the bush', which can be found in its current form as early as 1833, although forms of the proverb date back to the Bible translated into English by Wycliffe in 1382, and pubs of this name appear in the Middle Ages. The pub itself can be dated from about 1889, at which time dining rooms run by William Henry Shearmur were situated next door at No. 128. Miss Mary Ann McAuliffe ran the milliner's shop at No. 124.
(Photograph loaned to Tower Hamlets Local History Library and Archives by Truman's Brewery)

The Bridge House, 187 Tredegar Road, on the corner of Lefevre Road, pre-1970. A beer retailer can be traced on this site from 1876. When the Lefevre Walk housing estate was built in 1970, the pub was demolished. The concerns of pub culture are nothing new, and in 1915, an article appeared in the *East London Observer* highlighting the good work of Harley Street Congregational Church: 'A good deal of the misery and crime of East London is due to drink. It is appalling to see the crowds thronging the public-houses on a Saturday night.' *(Photograph loaned to Tower Hamlets Local History Library and Archives by Truman's Brewery)*

Opposite: Bomb damage caused by a Zeppelin raid to the Black Swan pub, Bow Road, Bromley-by-Bow, September 1916. A 100 kg bomb hit the pub, causing the floors to collapse into the basement. The Reynolds family, who had just gone upstairs to bed, were all found in the cellar after the explosion. Cissie Reynolds, aged 19, and her sister, Sylvia Adams, were found dead. Sylvia's 13-month-old daughter (also Sylvia) was found dangling by her clothes in the rafters but died later of shock. Their grandmother, Mrs Potter, was also killed. George Reynolds, aged 8, his 9-year-old brother Sydney and Sylvia's husband Henry Adams were injured. Four-year-old Harry Taylor was killed in the house next door to the pub, which was also destroyed.

Left: The ceremony of hanging up a hot-cross bun at the Widow's Son pub in Devon's Road. John Jackson, serving aboard HMS *Mercury*, is seen here hanging a bun in March 1964. The licensees at this time were Harry and Dorothy Prout. Legend has it that a widow lived here with her sailor son in a cottage on this site and, anticipating his return from sea, baked him a hot-cross bun for Good Friday. However, her son's ship was sunk in a storm. Every year from then on, the widow would bake a hot-cross bun for her son, never giving up hope that she would see him again. On the widow's death, the buns were collected together and strung from a beam in the cottage, which was soon nicknamed the Bun House. The tradition of hanging up a bun carries on today with one hung from the ceiling of the pub every Good Friday.

Below: The Widow's Son, also known as the Bun House, Devon's Road, *c.* 1952. The exterior has been much altered over the years.

The Bromley Arms, 51 Fairfield Road, 1981. The Bromley Arms serves as a typical example of the fate of many pubs in East London. It has recently undergone conversion and is now the Bromley Arms Apartments, situated in a prime location near to tube, bus and DLR stations as well as the Roman Road market. A public house had been in existence on this site since the 1850s. (*Photograph donated to Tower Hamlets Local History Library and Archives by Mrs Ely*)

Priory Tavern, 37 St Leonard's Street, 1990. This public house was named in memory of the priory of St Leonard, which was situated nearby. A pub had stood on this site since 1861, and was remodelled in the 1920s. The pub has been redeveloped and is now Mahee Court, a residential property. (*Photograph donated to Tower Hamlets Local History Library and Archives by Mrs Ely*)

The Addington Arms, 1974. The Addington Arms and Addington Road may owe
their name to the *Henry Addington*, the first ship to enter the West India Dock
after its opening in 1802. The Rt Hon. Henry Addington was one of the Lord's
Commissioners of the Treasury at the time.

The Caledonian Arms, 62 Fairfield Road, 1981. A beer seller had been located on
these premises since 1848. Fairfield Road was named after an annual Whitstable fair
that took place nearby. The fair, which began in the 1660s, had, by the nineteenth
century, gained a reputation for debauched behaviour involving rowdiness and
drunkenness. Unsurprisingly, the fair was forbidden in 1823. *(Photograph donated to
Tower Hamlets Local History Library and Archives by Mrs Ely)*

Right: The King's Arms, 167 Bow Road, 1982. Coachmen and wagon drivers used to stop outside the pub and water their horses at a trough. Like many other pubs, the King's Arms had a reputation for being haunted; its ghost reportedly had a habit of moving glasses around. The pub has been modernised but its gabled roof is a reminder of the time when the building stood in the old Bow village.

Below: The Imperial Crown pub, Talwin Street, April 1990. The flats in the background are in St Leonard's Street and were demolished in the mid-to-late 1990s. This view no longer exists due to rapid development in the area. The open space in the foreground of the photograph has been built over and the pub is now closed. *(Photograph donated to Tower Hamlets Local History Library and Archives by Mrs Ely)*

The Hand and Flower pub, Parnell Road, 1970. A public house has been on this site since about 1863. Parnell Road was constructed in 1873–4 and replaced Park Road, Park Road South, Park Road Terrace, Sidney Terrace, Argyle Terrace and Summer's Terrace. The offices of the East London suffragettes were situated nearby at 321 Roman Road.

4

Churches & Religion

Sketch of Stratford, Bow, 1818. St Mary's Bow Church can clearly be seen in the background. Workmen appear to be repairing Bow Road, which has been the main thoroughfare into Bow for centuries. A church has been present on this site since 1311 when the Bishop of London granted to the inhabitants a license to erect a chapel. Prior to this, those who wished to worship had to walk to the parish church of St Dunstan's in Stepney. In 1941, the Church of St Mary's was severely damaged by enemy bombing. Repairs in the brickwork can clearly be seen today.

Bow Road and the Church of St Mary, 1905. Although the origins of the church date back to the fourteenth century, the present building was built in 1719. This is when the church grew from a chapel of ease, serving a small community, to become a parish church. Prisca Coborn, a great benefactor to Bow, is buried at the entrance to the church. The statue of Prime Minister William Gladstone was erected in 1882 by Theodore Bryant of the Bryant & May match factory. The sculptor was Bruce Joy. It is one of the many myths of the East End that the financing of this statue originated partly from the wages of the matchgirls at Bryant & May. In protest, it is rumoured that the girls slashed their wrists and splashed their blood on the statue. This rumour led to a re-enactment of sorts in the 1990s when protesters, opposed to the redevelopment of the Bryant & May match factory in Fairfield Road into luxury flats, now known as Bow Quarter, splashed the statue with red paint. In fact, it was the drinking fountain in Bow Road, erected in October 1872 and now demolished, that was funded partly with deductions from matchgirls' wages. *(See page 110.)*

Above: An engraving of the Church
of St Mary with St Leonard, Bromley.
This church was demolished and
rebuilt in 1842–3.

Right: Interior of the Church of
St Mary with St Leonard, from
an engraving of 1852. All those
attending appear to be in their
Sunday best.

Above left: The rectory of St Mary's in the 1880s. This stood on the corner of Bow and
Fairfield Road where the National Westminster Bank now stands.

Above right: Vicarage in Bromley High Street. This building once belonged to Bow Brewery,
which was located nearby, and is now the site of Tudor Lodge. A double bedroom, top-floor
apartment in Tudor Lodge was advertised in July 2007 for £209,995. Such is the demand for
property in Bow and Bromley-by-Bow today.

Opposite above: The Church of St Mary with St Leonard, 1926. This church was built on the
site of what would have been the Lady Chapel of the Benedictine Priory of St Leonard, which
may well have been founded in Saxon times by St Dunstan. Geoffrey Chaucer certainly knew
of the priory and referred to it in his *Canterbury Tales*. The priory stood in about 16 acres of
land and the nearby River Lea would have served as a food source for the monks and nuns.
After the dissolution of the monasteries by Henry VIII, the Lady Chapel became Bromley's
parish church. The building, however, did not belong to the church authorities but to the
laymen who owned the Manor, and it was not until the 1890s that the Bishop of London
regained control of the church. The church remained in much the same form of the priory,
with some renovations and additions made. In 1843, the church was rebuilt by architect
William Railton, who was also responsible for St Bartholomew's Church, Bethnal Green, and
the Nelson Memorial in Trafalgar Square.

The Church of St Mary with St Leonard and the How Memorial Gateway, 1905. The ornate How Memorial Gateway, erected in 1894 in memory of Revd George Augustus Mayo How MA who served as vicar from 1872–93, stands today as the only evidence that a church was ever on this site. An article in *The London* in August 1896 reads: 'The parish church of Bromley is situated in the midst of a working-class population. Every parishioner seems to be employed in a factory or workshop. There is, of course, the usual "loafing" element, but it is not to be met with in Bromley so much as in districts further westwards. The houses are principally built in two storeys and are terribly monotonous. Most of them are let to two or three families.' The article goes on to publicise the work of Revd How's successor, Revd John Parry MA: 'Mr. Parry is a man of wonderful energy and resource. . . The social gatherings on his lawn for working men and women and factory girls and boys have done much to win the people to their vicar.' The church suffered considerable damage during the Second World War and was never rebuilt. The Blackwall Tunnel Northern Approach Road was built over the churchyard in the 1970s. The How Memorial Gateway now stands in silent tribute to the men and women who had, for centuries, served the people of the parish from this site.

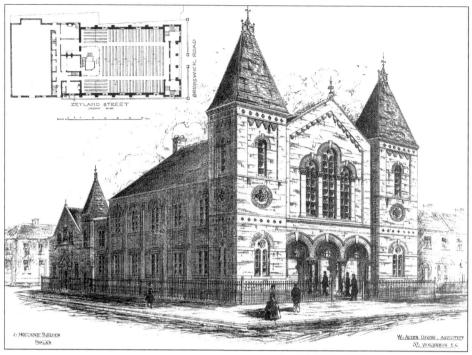

Poplar and Bromley Tabernacle as illustrated in *The Builder*, 11 August 1883. The Tabernacle was demolished in 1941 and ten years later was replaced with a modern building. Church halls were added to this building in 1958.

The exterior and interior of North Bow Congregational Church, which opened in Roman Road in 1867. The architect, Roland Plumbe, had an extensive practice specialising in working class housing and designed the Bryant & May match factory. The façade of this building still survives in Roman Road.

Above: An engraving of Bromley Chapel or Congregational Mission Church, Bromley-by-Bow, 1867. The architect of this chapel was Mr J.W. Norris. The church was destroyed by bombing during the Second World War and a new church was built in 1958 which, beside spiritual guidance, offered bread and soup to the locals during the winter.

Right: Lieutenant-Colonel G.E. Holman unveils the Bruce Provident Dividing Society's war memorial at Bruce Road Congregational Church, Bromley-by-Bow, September 1919.

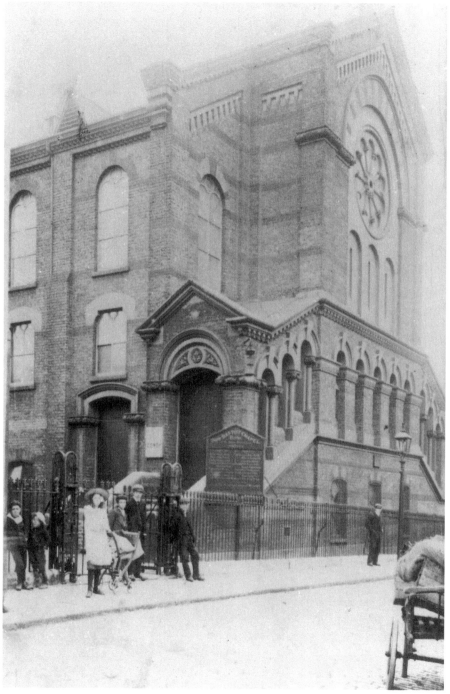

Bow Baptist Chapel, *c.* 1907. This building opened in 1866 and could seat 1,000 people. The cost was £7,000. An incendiary device destroyed the chapel during the Blitz in September 1940 but a new church and hall was built and opened on Bow Road in July 1957. *(Postcard loaned to Tower Hamlets Local History Library and Archives by Mr Philip Mernick)*

Bow Road Methodist Church, 3 June 1933. This was formerly Bow Road Wesleyan Chapel.

The stone laying ceremony officiated by Revd E. Benson-Perkins at the new Bow Methodist Church on 17 June 1950. The church was finally opened on 8 September 1951 and replaced one that was badly damaged during the second week of September 1940 – at the height of the Blitz – and was demolished in 1941. It became the first bombed Methodist church in London to be rebuilt after the war. Second from the left is Revd W.E. Clapham, minister of Bow Road Methodist Church from 1920–6 and 1930–54. During the 1930s, Revd Clapham wrote *The Good Fight at Bow* which described the work of the mission during the depression of the 1920s, which saw Bow and Bromley-by-Bow suffer mass unemployment and poverty. Methodism has a long tradition in the area and a Methodist chapel was established in the parish of Bromley St Leonard from 1779. John Wesley is known to have visited Bow on many occasions.

The minister of Bow Road Methodist Church, Revd Leslie Farmer with sisters of the Russian Orthodox Church, 1959. These sisters visited the church to sing carols. The sisters of the Russian Orthodox Church became refugees when Israel became an independent state and they emigrated to London.

St Michael and All Angels Church, St Leonards Road, Bromley-by-Bow, c. 1905. Dewberry Street is on the right. This church was built by R.W. Morris between 1864–5 and replaced a mission chapel that was built in 1861. In front of this now residential property is a white marble war memorial, built in 1920 by A.R. Adams, which shows the standing figure of Christ placing a wreath on a kneeling soldier in medieval dress.

St Stephen's Church, July 1953, on the occasion of the 96th anniversary service held at the church. Seen here is the Rt Revd Joost de Blank, Bishop of Stepney with mitre, with the Revd William H. Belcher, vicar of St Stephen's. On the far right is Revd N.C.P. Belcher, father of the vicar.

St Paul with St Mark, Old Ford, Bow. This church was first inaugurated in 1878. The church had to partly close in 1991 due to problems with funding. A major appeal was launched and more then £3m was raised from various sources including the National Lottery. The church's congregation also worked tirelessly, holding more than 271 jumble sales and raising over £20,000. Renovations began in March 2003. Three new floors of community facilities were built and the church now holds regular kids' clubs, keep-fit classes, a coffee shop, community events and exhibitions. *(Photograph donated to Tower Hamlets Local History Library and Archives by Mrs Ely)*

Above: Former Old Ford Methodist Chapel, Old Ford Road, *c.* 1971. This chapel was built in
1880–1 and closed in 1959. Old Ford Catering Equipment now trades on these premises.
This photograph, taken by Tower Hamlets architects department, was taken from Lefevre
Walk flats. Many changes have occurred in this area since this photograph was taken. Locton
Green, built in 1961 behind the former chapel, contrasts starkly with the reintroduction of
the traditional terraced two-storey houses with private gardens, after Lefevre Walk itself was
demolished in 2003. At the rear of the chapel can be seen the bus standing space which was
based there for many years. Next to the garage was a baby clinic in Rushton Street, built in
1937–8, and where the author went for his inoculations many years ago!

Opposite above: The Lighthouse Baptist Chapel, Devon's Road, *c.* 1982. Early in the 1860s,
Mr Tucker built 7 Glaucus Street. The surrounding area consisted mainly of market gardens
extending to Bow and Burdett Road. Meetings began at No. 7 where Revd J.R. Cox held Bible
readings and studies in the front parlour. When these became popular, the meetings moved
to a large disused room in River Street. The Lighthouse stands almost opposite the original
location of the front parlour meetings. *(Photograph donated to Tower Hamlets Local History
Library and Archives by Mrs Ely)*

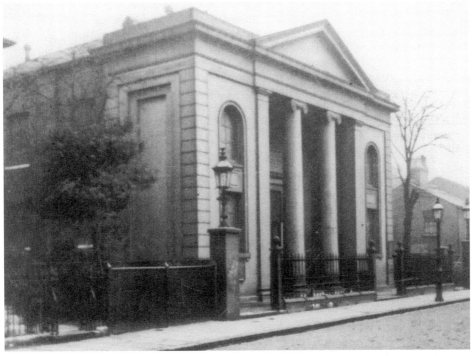

Harley Street Congregational Church, Bow. This church has gone through many changes in its existence. The building was originally built in 1854–5 as a Congregational Chapel which was converted in September 1927 into the Mile End and Bow District Synagogue. The synagogue held its final service in April 1977. Since 1979, it has been home to a Sikh Gurdwara Sangat. Harley Street was renamed Harley Grove in 1938. *(Postcard loaned to Tower Hamlets Local History Library and Archives by Mr Philip Mernick)*

Children's drill class, Harley Street Congregational Church, Bow. In 1915, Saturday concerts were held at the church in 'an attempt both to counteract the attractions of the public-house and to draw the people to the House of God.' The drill class was begun by a Mrs Keatinge and operated alongside other classes, including instruction in Morris and folk dances. Miss Grace Burby was in charge of the Girls' Club and Basket Class in 1915 and she spared, in the words of the *East London Observer* of 16 January 1915, 'an evening each week for training the somewhat exuberant spirits of the girls, and winning their affections for the highest and the best.' *(Postcard loaned to Tower Hamlets Local History Library and Archives by Mr Philip Mernick)*

5

Looking After the People

Staff and patients of B Ward, Poplar and Stepney Sick Asylum, *c.* 1910. The asylum became St Andrew's Hospital in 1925. *(Postcard loaned to Tower Hamlets Local History Library and Archives by Mr Philip Mernick)*

Above: Bow Vestry Hall, Fairfield Road. Built in about 1861, the hall became the Public Health Offices in 1936.

Below: Tower Hamlets Register Offices, formerly Bromley Vestry Hall, 1981. The Vestry Hall was built on the site of the Bowry Almshouses in 1878 but become obsolete when the boroughs of Poplar, Bethnal Green and Stepney were formed. Mary Bowry, the widow of a Captain Bowry of Marine Square, who died in 1715, left a bequest for eight almshouses to be erected for 'poor men who must have been bred to be seamen and to their widows past labour.' They were sold to parish officers in 1878 who then demolished them and built the Vestry Hall. The suffragettes held meetings at the hall but Poplar Council barred them from using it following increasing incidents of violence. At one incident in July 1913, police broke up a meeting and three suffragettes, Sylvia Pankhurst, Mrs Watkins and Mrs Ives avoided arrest by hiding in a nearby stable until four o'clock the following morning. Willie and Edgar Lansbury rescued them: Sylvia was tied up in a sack and placed in a wood cart, hidden under a pile of wood. She was then taken to a cousin of the Lansburys' in Woodford, Essex. *(Photograph donated to Tower Hamlets Local History Library and Archives by Mrs Ely)*

Bromley Public Hall, formerly Bromley Vestry Hall, on Bow Road. Opened on 27 May 1879, this photograph shows the hall floodlit in celebration of the coronation of King George VI in 1937.

Poplar and Stepney Sick Asylum, *c.* 1910. This building opened in 1871 for workhouse inmates who required medical attention. It was one of the earliest and largest workhouse infirmaries to be built following the Metropolitan Poor Act of 1867. Its pavilion plan became a model for other infirmaries. *(Photograph donated to Tower Hamlets Local History Library and Archives by the editor of the* East London Advertiser *in 1973)*

St Andrew's Hospital, Devon's Road, *c.* 1934. The hospital cost £43,000 to build plus £7,300 for the site. The architects were Arthur and C. Harston of Poplar. The hospital has now closed, and at the time of writing, is due to be redeveloped.

St Clement's Hospital, the old Bow Infirmary, Bow Road, 1960. This building opened as the City of London workhouse in 1848, becoming Bow Infirmary in 1874 and then Bow Institution in 1913. It was expanded into a hospital by the London County Council in 1932 and named St Clement's Hospital in 1936. A mental observation unit was established in 1933. Francis Hammond, architect to the City of London Guardians, added this central lodge with pedimented doorway in 1896. Patients were moved to Mile End Hospital in 2006–7 following the closure of St Clement's.

Poplar Municipal Hall and Poplar Civic Theatre, decorated for the coronation of Queen Elizabeth II in 1953. This building, also known as Poplar Town Hall, was opened on 3 December 1938 by George Lansbury and served as a replacement for Poplar Town Hall, Newby Place. The council had owned the land since 1926, but the costs involved had delayed the building of a centre which was to house all the council's staff under one roof. The new building cost £190,000, with the cost divided between £178,000 for the building and £12,000 for equipment and furniture. The interior furnishing consisted of officials' chairs made of steel and covered in red morocco leather and other furniture in walnut. It was also planned to have modern equipment in the offices including Dictaphones. The Assembly Hall could be arranged for stage performances and meetings and could accommodate 896 people on the ground floor and 446 in the gallery. The ground floor could also be cleared away to make room for dancing and had a sprung floor. There would also be an orchestra pit and dressing rooms. The design of the building was modern and caused some comment. *The Star* of 24 August 1937 reported that people were already calling the building 'a bacon factory' or coach station. The building was one of the first local authority buildings to try to attract the public and is in many ways the forerunner of today's Idea Stores. The *East End News* of December 1938 responded to the views of the Town Hall as a 'factory': 'What of it? In so far as a factory was a place where worthily by the work of man's head and hands the desires of his heart could be made living and fruitful that was what they wanted. That was why they were very proud of the new building.' On the frontage of this building are five panels carved in Portland stone. These panels depict the professions employed in the building of the hall: welder, carpenter, architect, labourer and stonemason, and were made by David Evans, who took sketches of the men working on the Town Hall on which to base his panels.

Above: The official opening ceremony of Poplar Town Hall, Bow Road, on 3 December 1938, conducted by the Rt Hon. George Lansbury MP, pictured here in the centre with his arm around his granddaughter, Angela Lansbury, the film, stage and television star. An opening dance was scheduled for the evening in 'London's Newest Ballroom' and there was a personal appearance by Stan Bloomfield's Harlem Band. The Mayors of twenty-three Metropolitan boroughs were among the guests at the opening. Also pictured here are the Mayor and Mayoress, Councillor and Mrs John F. Gilbertson and actress Moyna McGill, the second wife of Edgar Lansbury and mother of Angela. George Lansbury lived at 39 Bow Road from around 1920 until his death in 1940. The Lansbury family home was damaged during the Blitz and council housing was built on the site.

Opposite above: Bow police station and Addington Road, *c.* 1905. The first mention of a police station in Bow can be found in police orders of 1864. This referred to the station that originally stood at 116b Bow Road. The married quarters and section house stood on Violet Road but were demolished in the late 1970s. The police station in this photograph stands on ground purchased in 1901 from Lord Tredegar. Operation of these premises began on 20 July 1903. The suffragettes were frequent guests at this station during the period 1912–16. The building was restored following a direct hit during the Blitz. The station has a well-equipped stable, which in 1979, accommodated twenty horses and had its own forge and blacksmith. *(Photograph loaned to Tower Hamlets Local History Library and Archives by Revd A.R. Royall)*

Above: County Courthouse, Bow, *c.* 1908. This courthouse was designed by Charles Reeves and built in 1860. The Thames Magistrates Court and Juvenile Court, designed by Philip Arrand, architect to the Metropolitan Police, and built in 1990, now stands on this site in Bow Road opposite Bow Police Station. Bow County Court is now located in Romford Road.

Left: Bow Fire station, Parnell Road. Built in 1910 by W.E. Riley, architect to the London County Council, the station was opened on 19 May 1911 – the same day as Brunswick Road fire station. It housed a station officer, eleven firemen, a petrol motor fire engine, electric motor escape, manual fire escape and a horse cart. Due to the prevalence of industry in the area, Bow has always been in need of a fire service. Between 1848 and 1876, Old Ford Road saw three major fires break out: at Wentworth's Oil and Varnish Works in 1848, Hewett and Co. Soda Factory – resulting in the loss of one life – in 1874, and Robinson Cabinetmakers in 1876. The fire service was at the forefront during the Blitz which began on 7 September 1940. Hundreds of bombers flew over the East End, the first wave of bombs hitting the poorest and most overcrowded areas of London. By the second attack that same evening, 430 East Enders had died and 1,600 were seriously injured. Tens of thousands were made homeless. The date became known as 'Black Saturday'. By the end of May 1941, over 43,000 civilians had been killed and more than a million houses destroyed or damaged. *(Postcard loaned to Tower Hamlets Local History Library and Archives by Mr Philip Mernick)*

Above left: Laying the foundation stone for the Kingsley Hall Settlement, 14 June 1927. Actress Sybil Thorndike, whose career spanned six decades and who, incidentally, was the first British actress to appear on a postage stamp, is second from the left, and John Galsworthy, author of *The Forsyte Saga* and Nobel prizewinner for literature, is in the process of laying a brick. Two sisters, Doris and Muriel Lester, who had been involved in charitable work before the First World War, built the hall in memory of their brother, Kingsley, who died in 1914, aged 26. The hall was designed by the architect C. Cowles-Voysey, who also designed the Children's Home in Bruce Road in 1923, on behalf of the Lester sisters, and which was opened by author H.G. Wells. Doris Lester died in 1965 and Muriel Lester in 1968.

Above right: Kingsley Hall, Powis Road, 1975. This photograph shows the derelict hall before restoration in 1982–5, and which is still used as a community centre today. A publicity leaflet stated: 'opened 1915, bombed 1916, blasted 1940, still stands to enrich the common life of the people of Bow.'

Opposite below: Drapers Almshouses, Priscilla Road, *c.* 1900. These almshouses were built in 1706 for twelve poor persons. Four additional houses were erected in 1836. They are now private dwellings. The Draper's Co. is one of the twelve great companies of the City of London. The Mercers' Company is the premier company. The order was decided in 1515 when the Lord Mayor decreed the Mercers' as number 1. Two companies, the Skinners and the Merchant Taylors, would rotate in order annually; one would be number 6 and one number 7, except when the Mayor is a member of either company when that company would then get precedence. This is where the saying 'all at sixes and sevens' originates. There are 107 livery companies in the City of London today, all of which give considerable amounts to charitable causes every year.

Mahatma Gandhi at Kingsley Hall during his visit to London in 1931. While attending
the Round Table Conference held at St James' Palace to discuss the independence of India,
Ghandi turned down the offer of luxury accommodation in the West End, opting instead to
spend the entire three months of his stay at the hall, remarking that here, 'I am getting to
know people'. The hall was used again to recreate the visit during the filming of the Oscar-
winning film, *Gandhi* in 1981, staring Ben Kingsley. The activities of the hall were based on
an ashram, which Muriel Lester had encountered during her visit to Gandhi at Ahmedabad.
Income, housework other responsibilities were all shared. Standing in this picture are John
Dockes and Miss Slade. Gandhi is seated in the middle, and on the far right of that row is
Muriel Lester. George MacFarland is in the front row on the right. The legacy of welcoming
all was still in evidence in 1965 when the *East London Advertiser* stated that Kingsley Hall
'seeks no special age group. In fact everyone is welcome and newcomers are soon old friends.'
(Photograph loaned to Tower Hamlets Local History Library and Archives by Mrs C. Docker)

6

Education & Leisure

Children in Victoria Park, June 1957. This shallow lake was also used to sail model boats. The park was named after Queen Victoria and was built to improve the health of the overcrowded residents of the area. Although it was officially opened in 1845, the park was unofficially in use by the locals by 1843. The park has always been extremely popular, and 300,000 people visited the park during the Whitsun holiday on 6 June 1892.

Class VII, Old Palace School, Bromley-by-Bow, 1922. Some of these children, aged about seven, have been identified. They are, back row, from left to right: -?-, -?-, -?-, -?-, -?-, -?-, -?-, -?-, Phyllis ?, Bernard Lockett, Mildred Harris, Alice Strutton, Carrie ?. Third row: Robert ?, Ivy Williams, -?-, -?-, Grace ?, -?-, Teddy Lamb, Edith Morgan, Gwen ?, Ivy Smith, Alice Allen, -?-, -?-. Second row: -?-, Gwendoline Dowding, Miriam Mayes Cuff, Henrietta Barker, Edith Jackson, Ruby Pickett, Harriet Sykes, Kitty Macnamara, Ivy Monk, Mary McGuire, Emily ?. Front row: -?-, Tony Ellis, -?-, -?-, -?-, -?-, Leonard ?, -?-, Ivy Lockwood, Eileen Connolly.

During the Second World War, the school was used as a sub-station for the London Fire Brigade and the headquarters of the local rescue services. On the night of 19 April 1941, four service crews from Beckenham reported to the Old Palace School in response to one of the heaviest nights of bombing in London when the Luftwaffe dropped over 1,026 tons of high explosive and 153,096 incendiary bombs. Just before 2 a.m., Old Palace School received a direct hit, demolishing part of the building. Thirty-six firemen were killed, including all four of the Beckenham crews. A memorial plaque on the wall of the school serves as a tribute to these men and a reminder of the tragedy of war. *(Photograph donated to Tower Hamlets Local History Library and Archives by Mrs Carol Rackham)*

THE CRICKET GROUND, VICTORIA PARK

Above: Visitors to Victoria Park enjoying a game of cricket at the cricket ground. *(From a postcard loaned to Tower Hamlets Local History Library and Archives by Mr Philip Mernick)*

Right: Stone alcove from London Bridge, 1968. The bridge was demolished in the 1830s and this alcove, along with others, was moved to Victoria Park. The author remembers sheltering in the alcove many times when caught in the rain while cycling around the park. *(Photograph donated to Tower Hamlets Local History Library and Archives by K. Rayden)*

Grove Hall Park, 1972. Bow bus garage in Fairfield Road – built as London County Council's tram depot in 1907–8 and extended in 1910–11 – was built on some of the land of the largest mansion in Bow, Grove Hall. Built in the seventeenth century, this mansion was a lunatic asylum in the nineteenth century before it was demolished in 1909. A small part of the gardens can be glimpsed today as they were preserved in the form of Grove Hall Park.

Bromley House School, sometimes known as Bromley School or Bromley Manor House Academy, c. 1775. Teaching took place in what was formerly the Manor House of the Upper Manor of Bromley built by Sir John Jacob. The sketch was accomplished by General Frederick Maitland who attended the school from 1771 to 1779. In advertising to prospective pupils the positive aspects of the school, it was stated that 'the utmost salubrity of air, with the peculiar advantage of many acres of pleasure grounds, solely appropriated for the amusement of pupils, and entirely detached from every other communication.' The grounds the school covered were extensive, from the River Lea on the east, to what is now St Leonard's Street on the west, and on the south to Three Mills Lane. *(Donated to Tower Hamlets Local History Library and Archives by K. Rayden)*

Standard 3, St Leonard's Road School, May 1906. The headmaster, Harry Barge, is seated
on the left. This school was destroyed by enemy action during the Second World War. Its
replacement, Manorfield Primary School in Wyvis Street, Bromley-by-Bow, was designed by
Robert H. Matthew, architect of the Royal Festival Hall, and cost approximately £112,000.
The new school was designed to accommodate 680 primary school children. It was officially
opened on 19 March 1953, although it was being used before this date. It was opened by
Miss Marjorie Eele, who, in the words of the *East End News* of 20 March 1953, was famous
for her 'regular Music and Movement broadcasts to schools'.

Malmesbury Road School, *c.* 1905. This particular small corner of Bow situated to the east of Tredegar Road has not changed a great deal in the last hundred years. The school was damaged during the Second World War by enemy action and was repaired and improved at a cost of £11,530. One former pupil, Mr Will E. Sampson, who attended the school between 1910 and 1914, remembers the sweet and toyshop around the corner from the school and recollects purchasing a farthing kite and a bag of liquorice cuttings for a farthing. Other sweets for sale in the shop were sold at a halfpenny or a farthing for four ounces. How prices have changed!

A classroom at Bromley Hall Road School, *c.* 1913. Perhaps this was the first time some of the pupils had seen a camera, which may explain some of the expressions on their faces. This photograph was copied from an original loaned to Tower Hamlets Local History Library and Archives by Mrs Skeat, whose husband, Leonard Skeat, is third from the left in the third row, and Leonard's sister, Winnie, is second from the left in the front row.

High School, St Catherine's Convent, 181 Bow Road. The *East London Observer* of
1 August 1914 reported on the work of Father O' Gorman during the past year:

> They had formed commercial elocution classes, which had proved very successful.
> The great aim . . . of those engaged in education was the formation of character, and
> in that the parents could help very much. But many parents did not seem to realise
> that this could only be done by regular attendance at the school. He spoke also of
> the successes that had been gained in the examination for the College of Preceptors
> by two of the girls recently, and by others in commercial studies which, he said, were
> very important to them, as it was a good preparation for their future life. The power of
> speaking correctly was a great qualification.

An advertisement reports that the school's 'Course of Instruction comprises all the
ordinary subjects of English Education, French, Singing, and Drawing, a Commercial
Class, will be opened in September 1913. Typewriting and Shorthand will also be
taught.' *(Postcard loaned to Tower Hamlets Local History Library and Archives by
Mr Philip Mernick)*

High School, St Catherine's Convent. The pupils appear to be somewhat apprehensive in
this photograph; perhaps they were about to face a test in how to speak correctly! *(Postcard
loaned to Tower Hamlets Local History Library and Archives by Mr Philip Mernick)*

Pupils from Coborn School for Girls taking part in physical training in the school playground. Coborn School was opened by Princess Christian on 9 June 1898. The original site for the school was at the rear of St Mary's Church, Bow. In 1814 a new school opened in Fairfield Road. In 1892 it moved into the old Coopers Co. School for Boys at 86 Bow Road. The boys were educated at a school on a site at Tredegar Square and the girls at a Bow Road site. It owed its origins to Prisca Coburn (*née* Forster), born on 24 August 1622. She was the daughter of a minister of Bow Church, and at the age of 53, married Thomas Coborn, a wealthy brewer in Bow. Soon widowed, she was left with a brewery to run and a young stepdaughter. When she died in 1701, aged 80, her will stated that:

> the overplus of the said rents and profits be applied for the maintenance and support of some fitting and credible man, and his wife, who will take to teach and instruct the children Male and Female of such poor inhabitants of the said Hamlet of Bow, who shall not be of sufficient ability to give them learning and education at their own costs and charges, in the rudiments and principles of the Church of England, and shall teach the male children to read, write and cast accounts, and the female children to read, write and work at their needle, or otherwise as they find them qualified, and shall take care to have all the said children duly brought to Church to hear Divine Service and to have them frequently catechised whereby they may be brought up and educated in a virtuous way of living and fitted for some honest trades or employments.

In 1886, the chairman of the governing body of Prisca Coborn's Foundation Schools was Revd G.A.M. How of Bromley. The headmaster was Mr E. Stroud. Subjects taught in 1898 were English, Mathematics, Science, Drawing, Vocal Music, Latin, French and German. School fees covering tuition and the use of books and stationery were £2 per term for those aged 10 or over, and £1 5s for those aged under 10. An entrance exam was sat at noon and the term would begin on the same day at 2 p.m. Famous pupils included Elsie and Doris Walters, sisters of Jack Warner, stars of stage, radio and television, and Bernard Breslaw, who is most remembered for his roles in the *Carry On* films. One of the oldest girls' schools in London, Central Foundation Girls School, took over the Coborn School in 1975.

Harley College, 53 Bow Road, *c.* 1900. Harley College was the headquarters of the 'Regions Beyond Missionary Union'. This union offered training for medical missionaries who would then see service in Africa and the Far East. The headquarters had gone by 1923. *(Postcard loaned to Tower Hamlets Local History Library and Archives by Mr Philip Mernick)*

Unveiling ceremony of Marner Street School war memorial, Bromley-by-Bow, by the Rt Revd Bishop of Stepney on 31 January 1923. Headmaster Mr T.R. Rand is standing on the extreme right of the photograph. The memorial listed ninety-three former pupils of the school who died in the First World War. A local newspaper stated at the time that this was 'a splendid record for one school'.

Above: Infants' Class, St Leonard's Road School, 1913. Although this photograph has been numbered, the children remain unidentified. The schoolmistress was Miss Fosh.

Right: The original public library in Bromley St Leonard. This library was located at 126 Brunswick Road, on the corner with Abbott Road, and opened on 24 April 1895. The building ceased to be used for library purposes in 1906 and was demolished in the early 1930s.

Bromley Library, Brunswick Road (later Gillender Street). This library replaced the original public library at 126 Brunswick Road and was opened in May 1906 at a cost of £10,000. Leaside Regeneration bought the building, which closed as a library in 1991. Part of their work concerns conservation along the River Lea flowing near the Olympic Park.

Leading department counter, Bromley Library, *c*. 1912. Pictured in the photograph are William Benson Throne, librarian in charge, and his daughter Winifred. The thoughtful sign 'Silence is Requested' politely banned noise and gave the readers some respite to read without disturbance.

Right: Architect's plans of Passmore Edwards Library, Vernon Road, off Roman Road, *c.* 1900. In April 1896, a ballot of ratepayers took place and the overwhelming wish was for a library. Although there were problems finding a site in 1899, two shops opposite the baths in Roman Road were obtained for £1,575 and were demolished to make way for the library. The ground floor had a news reading room for thirty-three readers, and a lending library of 12,000 books. The first floor reference room had facilities for fifty-six readers and a reference book stock of some 5,000 volumes. £4,000 of the total cost of building the library (£6,000 total cost) was given by the former newspaper owner and benefactor, Passmore Edwards. In 1962, the new Bow Library in Stafford Road was opened and the *East London Advertiser* stated that 'the unattractive building in Vernon Road has issued its last book . . .' This was perhaps premature as the Bow Idea Store, with its multimedia facilities and library, now occupies the site.

Below: Bow Public Library, 1970. The author has spent many happy hours here browsing the shelves and borrowing books.

The opening of the extension to Bow Library on 11 February 1950. Four successive chief librarians of the borough of Poplar gather together with Mr C. Key MP, who is examining a book. From left to right are Mr H.M. Thompson, 1942–7, Mr R.F. Bullen, 1928–34, Mr W.B. Thorne, 1934–42 and Mr A.E. Pitt, 1948–58. Mr Key was Minister of Works but lost the post following the result of the General Election on 23 February 1950.

Opening of the new Bow Library in Stafford Road, 7 July 1962. Alderman C. Blaber JP is opening the proceedings. The Children's Library, where the author spent many happy hours as a child, can be seen in the background.

Above: Looking north from Vernon Road towards Bow Baths. These baths, formally located in Roman Road, contained slipper baths, a swimming pool, a public laundry and a hall for community meetings.

Below: Old Ford Picture Palace, 55 St Stephen's Road, *c.* 1912. This cinema was renamed the Ritz after the Second World War and was closed in 1961. One of the advertised films – *Making a Man of Him* – was released in 1912. Mr McDonnell, the proprietor, is standing on the far left.

Bow station, 1931. The station was built in 1870 and described by Pevsner as consisting of a 'front of nine bays, stock brick with giant pilasters, a kind of roundheaded Tuscan Trecento style'. It was demolished in 1975. The Bow and Bromley Institute, formed from the union of Bromley Literary Association and the Bow Working Men's Institute, was also based here and built as part of the station. In 1897, this institution became part of the East London Technical College, which closed in 1911. This site is now close to where Bow Church DLR station, opened in 1987, now stands. In 1871, a match tax was proposed by the government which consisted of ½d on each matchbox. Demonstrations against this tax were held in Victoria Park and a crowd marched to Westminster. Due to public pressure, the tax was withdrawn. To mark this event, Bryant & May built the ornate drinking fountain which was funded with public subscriptions and a shilling deduction from matchgirls' wages. The matchgirls referred to the fountain as being paid for 'with their blood'. Perhaps rather ironically, the fountain had a seated figure of Justice at its centre. The fountain was demolished in 1953 when the road was widened.

Children gather outside Bow Road station, possibly after returning from a group outing, or perhaps about to embark on one, *c.* 1900.

Bow station, North London Railway. Some of the architectural features on view here can still be seen on the platform of Bow tube station. The underground station was built in 1902 and is where the District line becomes an overground line when travelling west. Until the line was electrified in 1905, steam was the form of power used.

Old Ford station in the 1900s. This station, which was on the line running from Colchester via Romford, opened on 1 February 1865 and was renamed Coborn Road station on 3 March 1879. Perhaps this postcard was mailed by the same person who sent the one on page 26?

Coborn Road, *c.* 1909. The houses on the right of this photograph have been replaced with the Malmesbury West Estate. The bridge advertises the Coborn Road station, Great Eastern Railway, the entrance to which was just beyond the bridge. Initially the line ran from Bishopsgate, but a new terminus was opened at Liverpool Street in 1874. It was re-sited a short distance to the west in 1882 and opened in December 1883. It closed in 1916. George Lansbury joined campaigners to save the service, as fares cost 1½d compared to 4d for bus journeys into the city. The station reopened in 1919 but closed in 1946. *(Postcard loaned to Tower Hamlets Local History Library and Archives by Mr Philip Mernick)*

Coborn Road station, 1909. The increased use of omnibuses, trams and cars led to a decline in rail passengers in the inner suburbs. As well as Coborn Road, Bishopsgate Low Level and Globe Road also closed in 1916. The site is currently being redeveloped. *(Postcard loaned to Tower Hamlets Local History Library and Archives by Mr Philip Mernick)*

7

The People

Workers pose around an engine at locomotive sheds, Bromley sidings. The large number of women workers present in the picture indicates that it was probably taken during the First World War.

An early resident of Bow. A Roman coffin, aligned east/west, and a skeleton found at Old Ford on 22 May 1868.

Tower Hamlets cemetery, *c.* 1841. Established in 1841, this cemetery was the last of seven private cemeteries established in a ring around London. It advertised that 'A very eligible portion of the ground is set apart for Dissenters, and for whose accommodation every facility will be afforded.' The perpetual rights of burial in a family grave could be purchased for £3 3*s* or £2 2*s*. By 1851, some 5,000 people had been buried here, but reflecting the population explosion of the area and perhaps the hazards of the industrial age, this had risen to around 250,000 by 1889. Burials continued until 1966. The Greater London Council acquired the cemetery in 1965 and the cemetery chapels were demolished in 1972. A leaflet advertising the cemetery ends with the following intriguing sentence: 'In consequence of many mistakes having arisen, the Public are requested to notice, that this is the only Consecrated Cemetery in the Neighbourhood.'

George Lansbury talking to a matchbox maker's son in 1912. The boy is carrying the material for making matchboxes which he has collected from a factory. His family would spend many hours making the matchboxes, which would then be returned to the factory. George Lansbury, MP for Bow and Poplar, lost his seat in 1912. A highly principled man, he fought a by-election after stating he was in favour of women's suffrage, and resigned his seat so he could stand for re-election on the issue as an Independent. Lansbury was narrowly defeated. Many of his supporters were women who could not vote for him. In 1918, the law was changed, allowing more women than ever before the right to vote. *(Originally published in* George Lansbury: My Father *by Edgar Lansbury in 1934)*

Bow Mothers' Union, 1922. Mary Sumner, who formed the Union when her daughter, Margaret, had her first child in 1876, believed that the main responsibility of a good parent was to raise their child in the love of God. The first patron of the Union was Queen Victoria, and today it is now found in seventy-seven countries and has some 3.6 million members. The Union has been highly influential, reporting to the Royal Commission on marriage and divorce, and successfully campaigning to raise the minimum age of marriage for women to 16. *(Photograph loaned to Tower Hamlets Local History Library and Archives by Mr David Fielder)*

Workers pose outside the Bryant & May match
factory in Bow in the 1890s. The matchgirls would
form clubs known as 'feather clubs' and would
regularly pay a small amount into the club's funds.
When enough money was collected, they would
buy the best and most flowery hat they could
and share it between them. Who wore it on any
occasion probably depended, I am guessing, on
who had a date that evening. *(Originally published
in* Annie Besant: An Autobiography, *1893)*

Sylvia Pankhurst with one of her charges at the 'Mother's Arms', *c.* 1915. Sylvia
Pankhurst lived at 400 Old Ford Road, Bow, the headquarters of the East London
Federation of the Suffragettes. In April 1915, she took over the disused Gunmaker's
Arms, which was located on the corner of St Stephen's Road and Old Ford Road,
opposite Gunmaker's Lane. Here she established a Mother and Baby clinic, a crèche and
a Montessori School. The crèche received a great deal of support with grants from the
Corporation of London as well as the Ministry of Health and Education. This project,
known as the Mother's Arms, was a vital communal and political link for local women
in the First World War, while numerous men were away fighting, many never to return.
(Illustration from The Home Front, *Sylvia Pankhurst)*

16th Poplar (London) Scout Troop, *c.* 1915. Mr Eric Girton is standing directly behind the vicar, Revd Kitcat of St Mary's Church, Bow. He joined one of the many troops founded after the publication of *Scouting for Boys*, written by Lord Robert Baden-Powell. Within two years of the first camp at Brownsea Island in 1907, a rally at Crystal Palace attracted 11,000 Scouts.

This photograph was taken when many scouts or ex-scouts were fighting overseas. During the First World War, some 150,000 scouts served and 12 VCs were won. This included a VC for a scout who was with the Manor Park Troop, John 'Jack' Cornwell, who won, posthumously, a Victoria Cross for his actions onboard HMS *Chester* at the age of 16, during the Battle of Jutland.

2007 marked the hundredth anniversary of the founding of the scouting movement and the 150th anniversary of the birth of Lord Robert Baden-Powell, founder of the scouting movement. Before the founder died in 1941, he wrote the following message:

Dear Scouts,
If you have ever seen the play *Peter Pan* you will remember how the pirate chief was always making his dying speech because he was afraid that possibly when the time came for him to die he might not have time to get it off his chest. It is much the same with me, and so, although I am not at this moment dying, I shall be doing so one of these days and I want to send you a parting word of good-bye.
Remember, it is the last you will hear from me, so think it over.
I have had a most happy life and I want each of you to have as happy a life too.

I believe that God put us in this jolly world to be happy and enjoy life. Happiness doesn't come from being rich, nor merely from being successful in your career, nor by self-indulgence. One step towards happiness is to make yourself healthy and strong while you are a boy, so that you can *be useful* and so can enjoy life when you are a man.

Nature study will show you how full of beautiful and wonderful things God has made the world for you to enjoy. Be contented with what you have got and make the best of it. Look on the bright side of things instead of the gloomy one.
But the real way to get happiness is by giving out happiness to other people. Try and leave this world better than you found it and when your turn comes to die, you can die happy in feeling that at any rate you have not wasted your time but have *done your best*. 'Be Prepared' in this way, to live happy and to die happy – stick to your Scout Promise always – even after you have ceased to be a boy – and God help you to do it.
Your Friend
Baden-Powell

(Photograph donated to Tower Hamlets Local History Library by Mr D. Girton)

National Federation of Discharged and Demobilised Sailors and Soldiers, *c.* 1920. This was the Bow, Bromley and Old Ford Branch situated at 582 Old Ford Road and was the first branch of the organisation. It was run by Mr and Mrs Chapman. The need for this organisation was great, as the long opening hours testify to. The National Federation of the Discharged and Demobilised Sailors and Soldiers, along with other ex-servicemen organisations: 'The Great War', 'The National Association of Discharged Sailors and Soldiers', 'Soldiers' and 'The Officers Association' were amalgamated in 1921 to form the British Legion. Earl Douglas Haig was deeply concerned with the welfare of his ex-soldiers and was involved in the foundation of the Legion, which sold artificial poppies every year, baring the legend 'Haig's Fund' to raise funds and for wearing with pride on Remembrance Sunday. Haig was regarded as a hero of the war. When Field-Marshal Earl Haig of Bemersyde died on 29 June 1928, his state funeral was attended by many thousands of soldiers with more then 30,000 veterans following the coffin to its final destination at Dryburgh Abbey. It was only after the publication of Lloyd George's war memoirs in the 1930s, who was himself known to detest Haig, was the myth put forward of the 'Butcher of the Somme' and that Haig was an incompetent commander who had no regard for the lives of his men. This gained credence in the 1960s with the play and subsequent film, *Oh What a Lovely War*. *(Photograph donated to Tower Hamlets Local History Library and Archives by Joyce Chapman)*

A hero of Bromley-by-Bow: Arthur Lovell of Gale Street, seen here while serving in the First World War. During the Armistice Day of 1928, Arthur Lovell fell under the wheels of a lorry in Burgess Street and was killed as he saved 4-year-old Nancy Wales from being run over. Lovell, a costermonger, left a widow and seven children. To mark his heroism, Countess Haig unveiled a memorial to him at Bromley Public Hall in May 1929, and crowds gathered in the street to hear the ceremony which was broadcast to them via microphone. The Lovell Fund raised about £2,190 for his widow and children from around a thousand contributors. An anonymous donation covered the expense of the portrait which served as the centrepiece for the memorial and costs of the administration of the Lovell Fund. The memorial bears the inscription, 'Arthur Lovell. Love is indestructible. Its holy flame for ever burneth; From Heaven it came, to Heaven returneth.' *(Photograph from memorial service booklet donated by Mr L.R. Oakes)*

Just after midnight on 24 September 1916, a Zeppelin dropped one high explosive and five incendiary bombs on St Leonard's Street and Empson Street, Bow. Four two-storeyed houses were destroyed and many others suffered broken windows. Six people were killed in this attack and eleven injured. The bomb that fell in St Leonard's Street hit W. Lusty's timber yard and also destroyed a row of small houses. Among those killed were George Scott Jones (41), Harry Brown (54), Harriet Diewett (53) and Mary Lumas (74). Blanche Bradford later died from her injuries. Twenty-two other people were injured in this attack.

Air-raid shelter located under the railway arches, Arnold Road, Bow, *c.* 1939. These were the premises of J. O'Connor, cooper and barrel merchant.

Full-time women wardens outside Bromley Public Hall, Bow Road, 15 October 1941. Those identified in this photograph are fifth from the left Mrs O'Leary, eleventh from the left Mrs Lakey, fifth from the right Mrs Stewart, ninth from the right Mrs Watson and tenth from the right Mrs Margetts.

Workmen building a surface air-raid shelter in Archibald Street, Bow, *c.* 1940.

Temporary air-raid shelter constructed from steel and sandbags at Electric House, Bow Road, 1939. The gentleman on the right of the photograph seems to be aware of the shadow of war looming ahead and the costs involved.

Children evacuated from Southern Grove School, Bow at Wantage, Berkshire, 1939. All are carrying their gas masks. This photograph was one of many publicity photographs taken to promote the 'joys' of evacuation. The reality was often very different. *(Photograph originally published in* Caps and Gymslips *by Les Todd)*

Children line up to pass through the archway of the Fern Street Settlement, *c.* 1950. One child seems particularly happy to receive a 'farthing bundle'.

Children waiting patiently for the weekly distribution of 'farthing bundles' at the Fern Street Settlement, 1934. The archway in which children must pass through to be entitled to a 'farthing bundle' had the following words upon it`; 'Enter Now Ye Children Small; None Can Come Who Are Too Tall'. Any child who could pass under this archway, which is 4ft and 4½in high, would be given a gift. The Fern Street Settlement was founded in 1907 by Miss Clara Grant, who had become headteacher at the infants' school in Devon's Road in 1900. Inspired by the work of Canon Barnett at Toynbee Hall, she helped children in her school by giving them breakfasts and proper clothes, as well as boots. She devised the archway as a way of deciding who should be given a small gift as so many children came and she did not have the time to check their ages, weights, or residences. The gifts, also known as 'farthing bundles', consisted of surprise 'treasures' – beads, balls, marbles, dolls, shells, pictures and books. The pictures would be gathered from old Christmas cards sent in by people from all over the country. Queen Mary always sent her old cards which would then be recycled. Miss Clara Grant was inspired to adapt the ideas of recycling items into toys by old ones that were kept in a case in her living room. These toys included a piece of firewood wrapped in newspaper which became a doll, balls made of paper and old stockings tied with string which served as cricket balls. By 1949, the year of the death of Clara Grant, who died a few months after been awarded an OBE, the height of the arch was 4in more than it was in 1907, as the average east end child was taller. The ceremony has continued every year since, and the Settlement celebrated its centenary in 2007.

A tea party held in Tapley Street, Bromley-by-Bow, to celebrate the coronation of King George VI and Queen Elizabeth in May 1937.

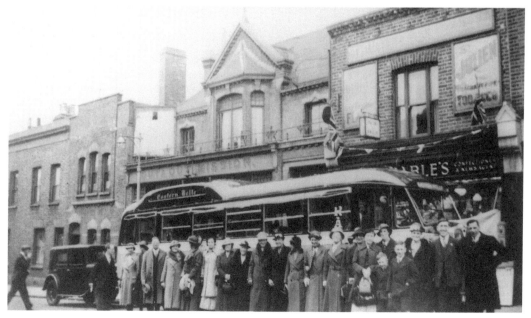

An outing on Whit Monday, 1937. This outing left from the 'Out and Out Mission' situated at Nos 181 and 183 Tredegar Road. To the right of the photograph can be seen Leonard Arthur Diable's, tobacconist and confectioners.

Celebrations in Barchester Street, Bromley-by-Bow, for the silver jubilee of King George V and Queen Mary on 6 May 1935. *(Photograph donated to Tower Hamlets Local History Library and Archives by Gordon Heath)*

Parnell Road, Bow, 1953. 'Miss Parnell' and a band of followers in Poplar's Coronation Carnival.

Crowds gather outside Bromley
Vestry Hall, Bow Road, for a glimpse
of the royal couple on their East End
tour, 3 June 1953.

ACKNOWLEDGEMENTS

T hanks go to the following people: Christopher Lloyd at Tower Hamlets Local History Library and Archives, for his advice, immense knowledge of the area, professionalism and for finding the time to help with this publication – his books inspired me to write my own East End history publications; Malcolm Barr-Hamilton, Tower Hamlets Archivist, for his friendship, pub chats, advice and support, and for needing a volunteer back in 1998; Sally Jacobs, Assistant Local Studies Officer at Tower Hamlets Local History Library and Archives, for her support; Steven Williams and Wendy Teo of Slapstick Design for their friendship and help, both professionally and personally – my Mum will keep supplying you (or should I say Steven) with cakes!; Dr Peter Catterall for his friendship and for finding the time to encourage and support me when the doubts crept in; Dr John Gardener for his advice, friendship and supportive email correspondence; Roy Sully and Shirley Day for their continued support and for Roy's valuable guidance when it came to the world of livery companies; Ms Raya McGeorge, a good friend and one of the most professional and dedicated archivists I know; Bob Stewart for his help and support in the early version of this book; Alfred Gardner and Linda for their continued friendship and support to me and my family; Elizabeth Tardios, an intelligent and inspirational woman whose smile makes the world a better place to live – thank you for being you; John Porter and family, for his friendship since university and for our infamous pub chats; Pia Crowley for her help and support, and for being there when I needed someone to listen; Lord Robert Baden-Powell for his friendship and supportive words; Alan Morgan for his friendship and for giving my voice its first role; Amy Rigg for her friendship since university, albeit from a distance, but we will catch up eventually; Lauren Banasky – a wonderful person, a friend and an inspiration; Philip Mernick for his encouragement and permission to use some of the images sourced from his wonderful postcard collection; Rosemary Taylor for her work in this area which was invaluable in the compilation of this volume; Matilda Pearce at Sutton Publishing for commissioning this work and for encouraging me.

Final thanks go to everyone who has donated photographs to Tower Hamlets Local History Library and Archives, 277 Bancroft Road, London, E1 4DQ. There are many fascinating stories of the East End to be discovered in this collection; please visit and discover them.